Carmit Rachel Swed

The Garden of Lost Balls

Illustrated by: Tamar Lenchner

Carmit Rachel Swed
The Garden of Lost Balls

All Rights Reserved
Copyright © 2022

Illustrations: Tamar Lenchner
Design and Graphics: Lior Naim
Translation and Editing: Dr. English

**I dedicate this book to my mother, Tehila Swed –
may she rest in peace.**

From the bottom of my heart I'd like to thank
the people who supported me, who shared and
participated in this publication, including:

Gideon Swed, Laura Swed, Limor an Rafi Oren, the
Filderman family, Einat Feldman, Bracha Franzus
Benayun, Liron Lieber, Daphna Genosar Levy, Att.
Ron Cahana, Orli Halevi.

Anna had a big, shiny blue ball.

Every day after school she'd play with the ball.
Sometimes she played with it at home,
sometimes at the playground.
Sometimes she played with friends,
and sometimes with the cats in the yard.

5

Anna loved her blue ball so much
that she never put it aside,
not even for a moment.
She even took it for a walk in a stroller,

ate her meals with it,
and slept with it in her bed.

One day, as Anna was playing with the ball,
throwing it high in the air,
the ball bounced, rolled away and ran off
beyond the playground, into the street.

8

Anna ran over to Mommy and asked her
to help get the ball back.

Mommy and Anna
hurried to search
for the ball,
but it was gone.
Anna looked
to the right again,
and again to the left –
but the ball was gone.
"Where is my ball? I
want my ball!"
Anna cried.

"I really don't know," Mommy replied.
"Maybe it was hit by a car,
maybe it was popped and deflated,
maybe it rolled down the street and disappeared...
The ball, my sweet Anna, is lost."

Anna started crying even harder.
"I want my ball," she sobbed,
and the tears fell from her eyes like rain.

Anna was very sad.
Anna was worried.
She didn't know what happened,
and was afraid of what might happen.
Who would look after her beloved ball?
Who would care for it?

At night, when she went to bed,
Anna was so worried she couldn't fall asleep.
Anna was very sad without her ball,
and her tears that had already dried started falling again.

Mommy came and sat by Anna's bed.
"Mommy, where do you think my ball is right now?"
Anna asked and sniffled.

Mommy hugged her and said:
"Oh, that's obvious, your ball is in the Garden of Lost Balls."
"The Garden of Lost Balls?" Anna asked.
"Yes," replied Mommy.

"In the Garden of Lost Balls,
you can find all the balls that were lost
and will never return.
They're having a good time in the Garden,
and they're happy. They're played with,
and only good things happen to them."

"Take me now to the Garden of Lost Balls," cried Anna.

"Sweetie, we don't have to go anywhere,"
Mommy answered.

"The Garden of Lost Balls is always with us.
It's in our hearts and minds,
 and whenever we want,
we can close our eyes and see
 all the lost balls."
"Really?" Anna asked, and stopped crying.

"Yes, really," Mommy said.
 "If you want to, my sweet Anna,
you can dream of the Garden of Lost Balls,
and play with your ball there."

That very night, when Anna fell asleep,
she arrived in her dream
at the Garden of Lost Balls.
Just as Mommy had promised,
she saw lots and lots of balls there,
in all sizes and colors,
and among them was her shiny blue ball.

18

Anna caught the blue ball,
and threw it with the greatest joy.

The next morning, right after brushing her teeth,
Anna told Mommy that she dreamed last night
of the Garden of Lost Balls
and played with her blue ball.

Now Anna isn't as sad.
She knows the blue ball is happy in the Garden,
and that she can visit it there every night.

Why and how should we talk with our child?

"Mommy, when I grow up, will you not be here (alive)?"
For the past six months I've been watching my five-year-old son, and realizing that he's starting to get a grasp of the concepts of "death" and "the end of life". At first he asked subtle, indirect questions, but later on they became direct and pointed.
As a professional who specializes in trauma, I've noticed that most parents choose to ignore these questions, suppressing them and waiting for another, later time, or maybe never. These questions concerning the subject of death stem from curiosity, and point to standard emotional cognitive development.

Avoiding a response to those questions leaves the child at a loss, lacking confidence and becoming profoundly more anxious.
However, an open and candid discourse allows for the expression of emotions, the manifestation of fears, and the asking of questions. Genuine age-appropriate dialogue gives the child the feeling that they are being listened to, cared for and trusted, and that their parents wish to help them cope with this issue.
The book can be read multiple times, and each time new questions and issues may arise from the point of view of different characters or different motifs, such as Anna, the ball she cares for, her mother, the Garden, and who/what can be found there.

Each page allows us to stop and look at the characters, their expressions and surroundings, and ask the following questions:
•   I wonder what Anna is feeling now that she's lost her ball? (angry/sad/scared/frustrated)
•   Do you also have something or someone that's dear to your heart? (person/object)
•   Did you ever lose anything or anyone? How did you feel? (longing/sadness/worry)
•   How does the Garden of Lost Balls seem to you?
         (Note the facial expressions of the characters in the garden).
•   I see that Anna has calmed down after dreaming about the Garden of Lost Balls. I wonder why
         (in the dream she sees that it's good, everybody's happy and smiling and are cared for...)

I recommend this book as an effective, useful tool suited
 for explanation and discussion of the child's growing understanding
of the concepts of death and loss.

Inbar Feuerstein, M.S.W, family, therapist,
 specializing in trauma care.

CPSIA information can be obtained
at www.ICGtesting.com
Printed in the USA
BVHW010833150323
660486BV00002B/40

9 789655 982831